The SAFe Practice Guide: Agile Transformation Using the Agile Release Train

Mark Heller

Published by Mark Heller, 2023.

While every precaution has been taken in the preparation of this book, the publisher assumes no responsibility for errors or omissions, or for damages resulting from the use of the information contained herein.

THE SAFE PRACTICE GUIDE: AGILE TRANSFORMATION USING THE AGILE RELEASE TRAIN

First edition. July 24, 2023.

ISBN: 979-8215240298

Written by Mark Heller.

The SAFe Practice Guide

Agile Transformation Using the Agile Release Train

Mark Heller

Disclaimer

The information in this book has been researched and prepared to the best of our knowledge and belief. It is for informational purposes only and does not constitute advice. Although I have taken great care to provide accurate and up-to-date information, I assume no liability for errors, omissions, or inaccuracies in the contents.

It is important to note that the implementation of the procedures and methods mentioned in the book depends on individual conditions and circumstances. Each organization and context is unique, and it is the reader's responsibility to adapt the information to their specific needs and take appropriate precautions.

I assume no liability for damages that arise directly or indirectly from the implementation of the procedures and methods mentioned in the book. Any application of the contents is at your own risk. It is recommended to contact qualified professionals or experts for individual advice in case of specific questions or concerns.

Please note that the business and technology landscape is constantly evolving, and it is possible that some information in the book may become outdated over time. I make no commitment to update the content to reflect changes or developments.

The disclaimer extends to all content, resources and recommendations contained in this book. It is the responsibility of the reader to critically review and independently evaluate the content.

By reading and using this book, you agree to this disclaimer.

The author

Recommendations for the introduction of ART

Foreword

Dear Readers,

I am pleased to present my developed book on the Agile Release Train (ART) and the Scaled Agile Framework (SAFe). This book is the result of my passion for Agile methodologies and my deep understanding of the challenges of scaling Agile practices in large organizations.

At a time when companies are increasingly turning to agility to adapt to rapidly changing market demands, it is essential to find scaling solutions that preserve the flexibility and efficiency of agile teams. This is where the Agile Release Train concept comes in, providing a structured and coordinated way of working to synchronize teams at the enterprise level and increase overall performance.

This book provides you with a comprehensive introduction to the Agile Release Train and its role within the Scaled Agile Framework. You will learn about the various roles and responsibilities necessary to successfully implement and operate the ART. In addition, I will provide you with detailed insights into the processes, activities and methods that can be applied within the ART.

I will also address the challenges you may face when implementing ART and share proven solutions and recommendations for implementing ART in your organization. I will encourage you to start your own journey to agility and take advantage of the Agile Release Train to take innovation, collaboration and customer satisfaction to a new level.

I am committed to making this book accessible to a broad readership, whether you already have experience with Agile or are just diving into the world of Agile. I have endeavored to explain complex concepts in an understandable way and to provide practical examples to make it easier for you to implement ART in your own organization.

I hope that this book will provide you with valuable insights and inspiration to help you successfully navigate the challenges of agile scaling. I would like to thank all those who supported me during the writing process, whether through technical expertise, helpful feedback, or encouraging words.

Now I invite you to join me on an exciting journey through the world of the Agile Release Train. May you gain new insights, expand your agility and align your organization for a successful future.

With best regards,

Mark Heller

Chapter 1: Introduction

We begin our journey in a place everyone knows well: the beginning. In Chapter 1, we welcome you to the world of the Scaled Agile Framework (SAFe). A world where agility, collaboration, and continuous improvement have become the critical drivers for successful organizations.

The rapid digital transformation and increasing globalization of markets have radically changed the way we work and do business. Large organizations face the challenge of adapting their business models and ways of working to stay ahead of the competition. This is where SAFe comes in.

SAFe is a proven, codified method for scaling agile principles and practices at the organizational level. It provides a structured but flexible approach that enables organizations to respond to the ever-changing demands and challenges of today's business world.

Our book will guide you step by step through the different aspects and concepts of SAFe. Whether you are an experienced agile practitioner or a newcomer to the agile world, we have made sure that this book is accessible to a wide audience. We will highlight both the theory behind SAFe and its practical application to give you a comprehensive understanding of this powerful framework.

We start with the basics, explaining the key principles and concepts of SAFe, and then move on to more specific topics such as the different roles in the Agile Release Train, the processes and workflows within the framework, risk and dependency management, and more.

It is our goal to not only provide you with the knowledge you need to implement SAFe in your organization, but also to give you the tools and techniques you need to drive sustainable agile transformation.

From the first page to the last, we want this book to be a source of inspiration, insight, and guidance for you as you embark on the exciting journey of agile transformation. Welcome to the first chapter of your SAFe journey!

Agility and its importance

Agility represents a key competitive advantage in today's fast-paced world, especially in industries such as software development and IT. At its core, agility is a mindset and approach to managing change and uncertainty in a complex environment.

Agility refers to the ability to respond quickly, efficiently and effectively to change and to manage it proactively. It involves a flexible, adaptive approach that enables changes to be used as opportunities for improvement, rather than seeing them as threats or obstacles.

The term "agility" originates from software development and was first formally defined in the "Agile Manifesto" of 2001. The Agile Manifesto sets out four core values and twelve principles that define the agile approach. Among other things, these values and principles emphasize the importance of individual and team-oriented processes, functional products, customer collaboration, and the willingness to respond to change.

In practice, agile encompasses a range of methods and practices, including Scrum, Kanban, and Extreme Programming (XP), based on the principles of the Agile Manifesto. These methods enable teams to work in short, iterative development cycles called "sprints" or "iterations." This iterative approach allows the team to quickly gather feedback and make changes, increasing product quality and customer satisfaction.

In recent years, agile has spread far beyond software development and is now being used in many other areas, including product management, marketing, human resources and more. This broad application demonstrates the growing importance of agility in the modern business world.

In summary, agile is much more than a methodology or a set of tools. It is a mindset and a culture that promotes flexibility, continuous learning, improvement and collaboration. It is a critical enabler for success in today's complex and ever-changing business environment.

Presentation of SAFe

SAFe stands for "Scaled Agile Framework." It is a framework developed and implemented by Scaled Agile, Inc. This framework enables companies to apply and manage agility on a large scale, typically at the level of entire organizations or large projects. SAFe thereby bundles proven concepts and practices from Lean Thinking, Agile Development, DevOps and more.

In its structure, SAFe comprises four configuration levels: Essential, Large Solution, Portfolio, and Full Configuration. Each of these levels addresses specific aspects of agile and lean thinking, depending on the size and complexity of the organization or project. For example, the Essential level focuses on team and program activities, while the Portfolio level addresses strategy and investment funding.

A key component of SAFe is the Agile Release Train (ART). The ART is a long-term, self-organized group of Agile teams that plan, commit, and work together on value streams. In the context of SAFe, a value stream is a series of steps an organization takes to deliver customer value. An ART delivers value to its stakeholders incrementally and on a regular basis, in what are called Program Increments (PIs).

SAFe aims to improve alignment, collaboration, and delivery across multiple Agile teams by scaling agility. It helps organizations respond faster and more effectively to market changes, increase productivity, improve quality, and increase employee engagement.

It is important to note that SAFe is not a rigid set of rules or procedures, but rather a flexible guide that can be adapted to the specific needs and circumstances of each organization. The key to success with SAFe lies in its proper adaptation and application, tailored to each organization's unique context and specific goals.

SAFe's place in the Agile world

SAFe has earned a remarkable place in the world of agile, especially when it comes to scaling agile practices in large organizations. While frameworks like Scrum and Kanban are great for smaller teams and projects, SAFe offers a comprehensive approach to managing the complexity that comes with adopting agile practices in larger organizations.

SAFe integrates several agile and lean principles and methods. It pulls elements from Scrum, Kanban, Lean Software Development and the DevOps mindset. This makes it a versatile and comprehensive framework that enables agility to be coordinated at different levels within an organization. It focuses on alignment, transparency and program execution across numerous teams and departments.

Another aspect that gives SAFe a unique place in the Agile world is its emphatically pragmatic approach. SAFe is designed to be adaptable to different organizational structures and sizes as needed. It provides not only a framework for execution, but also concrete advice and tools for its implementation and adaptation.

However, it is important to note that applying SAFe is not a panacea and successful enterprise-level Agile requires a deep shift in culture and mindset. While SAFe can be a powerful tool for navigating this change, success ultimately depends on an organization's ability to understand and apply the underlying principles of Agile and Lean Thinking.

Overall, SAFe is a highly respected approach to scaling agility in the Agile world. Through its comprehensive integration of various principles and practices, its adaptability, and its focus on pragmatism, it provides organizations with a solid foundation to successfully implement and manage agile at scale.

Description of the book structure

This book has been structured to provide a clear and comprehensive overview of the Scaled Agile Framework (SAFe) and the Agile Release Train (ART). It is structured to provide a wealth of information and insight for both newcomers to the world of SAFe and experienced practitioners.

The book is divided into three main parts:

Introduction: This part provides a general introduction to the world of agile, the importance and role of SAFe, and the structure of the book.

Agile Release Train in detail: This part is the core of the book and is dedicated in detail to the Agile Release Train (ART) within SAFe. Here, the roles, processes, activities, and methods related to the ART are examined in depth. Both theoretical aspects and practical use cases and examples are presented.

Connections and dependencies: This part explores the connections and relationships between the ART and other elements of SAFe, and how it fits into the broader Agile landscape. This understanding of the interconnections and dependencies is central to the successful application and implementation of SAFe at the organizational level.

Each chapter within these parts contains a carefully curated mix of theoretical explanations, practical examples, and advice to give readers a deep understanding of the topics covered. In addition, key points and summaries are provided at the end of each chapter to consolidate and reinforce what has been learned.

This book structure provides a methodical and structured approach to address the broad and complex topic of agile at scale using SAFe. It enables readers to familiarize themselves with the concepts and practices step by step and thus build a solid foundation for the practical application of SAFe and the Agile Release Train.

Chapter 2: SAFe Basics

Welcome to Chapter 2, where we embark on an in-depth exploration of the Scaled Agile Framework (SAFe). SAFe is a comprehensive yet flexible framework developed to implement the principles and practices of agile and lean management in large organizations. It provides a systematic approach to introducing ways of working based on agile principles at scale.

Let's start with the basic principles of SAFe. At its core, SAFe is based on nine fundamental principles that come from lean product development and agile thinking. These principles, which include a focus on cross-value stream teams, enabling rapid feedback cycles, and decentralizing decision making, form the basis for designing and applying SAFe in an organization.

A key aspect of SAFe is its layered structure, which consists of four configurations: Essential, Large Solution, Portfolio, and Full. Each of these configurations builds on the previous one and adds further elements relevant to larger and more complex organizations.

At the most basic level, the Essential SAFe configuration, we find the Agile Teams and the Agile Release Trains (ARTs). These are the heart of SAFe and continuously deliver valuable results implemented in small increments.

In the Large Solution configuration, an additional layer is introduced to manage large and complex solutions that exceed the capacity of a single ART.

The Portfolio configuration brings strategic management and governance into play, while the Full configuration combines all these elements and is suitable for the largest and most complex enterprise environments.

But SAFe is not just theory. It provides concrete tools and practices that help turn these principles into reality. From PI planning to Kanban methodology to continuous delivery, SAFe provides a framework that helps address product development challenges at scale.

It is important to understand that SAFe is not a rigid set of rules that should be adopted without customization. Instead, it serves as a guide that can be adapted and optimized by each organization to meet its specific needs and challenges.

Throughout this chapter, we will look in more detail at the different aspects of SAFe to give you a solid foundation for your understanding and to help you identify the opportunities that SAFe can bring to your organization. Welcome to the world of SAFe!

SAFe Principles

SAFe is driven by a set of core principles based on concepts from Lean Thinking, Agile Development, Systems Thinking, and DevOps. These principles are the foundation of SAFe and guide the decisions in the various SAFe practices and techniques. There are ten SAFe principles in total:

Adopt an economic point of view: This principle emphasizes that decisions should be made based on their economic value. This requires an understanding of cost, value, time and risk in decision making.

Apply systems thinking: This principle emphasizes the importance of looking at the system as a whole, not just its parts. It emphasizes that the behavior of a system is not determined solely by the behavior of its parts.

Embrace uncertainty and establish flexibility: This principle recognizes that plans and requirements may change over time and calls for flexibility in dealing with those changes.

Builds incrementally with fast, built-in learning cycles: this principle underscores the value of short feedback loops to quickly detect and fix defects and improve products.

Base milestones on target state evaluation: this principle recommends basing milestones on objective evaluations of the current state rather than on pre-planned dates.

Visualize and limit WIP, reduce batch sizes, and manage queue lengths: This principle emphasizes the importance of controlling the amount of work in the system to improve lead time and quality.

Apply variability thinking: This principle recognizes that high variation in early stages of the value creation process enables discovery and innovation, while low variation in later stages ensures reliability and efficiency.

Promote intrinsic motivation of knowledge workers: This principle emphasizes the importance of creating an environment that promotes autonomy, mastery, and purpose for knowledge workers.

Decentralize decision making: This principle recognizes that decisions are best made by those closest to the work.

Organize around value creation: This principle emphasizes the importance of aligning the organizational structure to create customer value.

These principles guide all activities performed within SAFe and are critical to understanding and effectively implementing the SAFe framework.

SAFe values

The values of a framework like SAFe are deeply held beliefs that guide behavior and decision making within the organization. SAFe emphasizes four core values that are central to the implementation and execution of the framework. These values form the backbone of SAFe and inform every facet of its application.

Alignment: SAFe emphasizes the importance of clear alignment of all teams and individuals to the common goals and vision of the organization. This means that all efforts and resources are focused on achieving these common goals. Alignment enables teams to work in sync and achieve results together.

Built in Quality: In SAFe, quality is not an afterthought, but an integral part of every activity and process. This means that quality is built into every phase and aspect of the workflow, from requirements gathering to development to delivery and maintenance.

Transparency: SAFe emphasizes the importance of transparency in the provision of information, decision-making, and work processes. This creates an environment of trust where issues can be openly addressed and resolved. Transparency also enables better decisions because they are based on complete and accurate information.

Program execution: SAFe places great emphasis on the actual delivery of valuable results. This means that while theory and planning are important, the ultimate focus is on implementing and delivering solutions that work.

These four values of SAFe are not just theoretical concepts, but are to be implemented and lived in practice. They guide the behavior and decisions of individuals and teams within a SAFe framework and form the basis for building a strong and effective Agile culture.

The four levels in SAFe

SAFe organizes work into four main levels to manage the complexity of the work while ensuring the participation of all necessary roles. These levels are:

Team level: This level includes the teams that do the actual work. In SAFe, these are Agile teams working in Scrum, Kanban, or other Agile methodologies. These teams develop increments of functional software in recurring iterations and are the foundation for the value stream in the SAFe framework.

Program level: This level includes the Agile Release Train (ART), which consists of multiple teams working together to achieve a common vision. At this level, the teams' efforts are synchronized to deliver new software versions (releases) at regular intervals, typically every ten weeks.

Large Solution level: This level comes into play when solutions are so large and complex that they require the coordination of multiple ARTs. Here, the efforts of multiple ARTs, as well as any necessary specialized teams, are coordinated to jointly develop a large, integrated solution.

Portfolio level: The top level in SAFe is the portfolio level. This is where strategic decisions are made and where programs and large-scale solutions are aligned. This is also where the funding and management of the value-creating initiatives (Epics) takes place.

These four levels enable team-level agility to scale across the enterprise. Each level has specific roles, artifacts, and processes to ensure coordination and synchronization between levels. Together, they form the SAFe House of Lean-Agile, a model that represents both the structure and dynamic interactions within a SAFe implementation.

Core components of SAFe

SAFe is a complex framework based on a set of core components. These components are critical to understanding and applying SAFe and help put the entire system in context. Below are some of the core components of SAFe:

- Agile teams: These are the basic building blocks of SAFe. They typically consist of 5 to 9 members and work in Scrum, Kanban, or another agile method. They work in iterations to deliver increments of valuable software.

- Agile Release Trains (ARTs): ARTs are groups of agile teams (typically 5 to 12 teams) that work together to achieve a common goal. They deliver incremental value in the form of Program Increment (PI) releases, typically every 10 weeks.

- Lean-Agile Leadership: Leaders play a critical role in SAFe. They drive transformation, promote alignment, build an environment of trust and innovation, and foster a learning and improvement mindset.

- Solution Trains: When a solution is so large that it requires the collaboration of multiple ARTs, a Solution Train is formed. This organizes the efforts of multiple ARTs and specialized teams to develop and deliver a large, complex solution.

- Portfolio Management: At the highest level of SAFe, the management of the project portfolio takes place. Here, the strategic goals and visions of the company are defined and resource allocation, epic management and financial management are performed.

- Lean budgets and guardrails: In SAFe, financing is performed on a portfolio basis using lean budgets. Financial guardrails are used to manage spending in line with business objectives.

Together, these core components of SAFe form a comprehensive framework to support organizations in today's volatile, uncertain, complex, and ambiguous (VUCA) business environment. They enable organizations to respond quickly and effectively to change and continuously deliver value.

Roles in SAFe

A key aspect of the SAFe framework is the definition of roles at each level of the organization, from the agile teams to the portfolio level. Each role has specific responsibilities and activities that contribute to the effective functioning of SAFe. Some of the main roles in SAFe are described below:

- Team member: Team members are the primary performers in agile teams. They work in cross-functional teams to deliver incremental value in each iteration.

- Product Owner (PO): The PO is responsible for prioritizing the backlog items and providing context for the team to work effectively. The PO is the liaison between the stakeholders and the team.

- Scrum Master (SM): the SM serves the team by removing obstacles, helping the team deliver quality work, and coaching the team in the application of Scrum and Agile practices.

- Release Train Engineer (RTE): The RTE is the Scrum Master for the Agile Release Train (ART). He or she coordinates the teams, assists with risk management, and helps ensure alignment with Program Increment (PI) goals.

- Product Manager (PM): The PM is responsible for providing context for the ART and helps prioritize the backlog items at the program level. The PM works closely with the Product Owners and Stakeholders.

- System Architect/Engineer: This role is responsible for defining and communicating the technical vision of the system and ensuring that all teams are working in alignment with that vision.

- Solution Train Engineer (STE): The STE is the Scrum Master for the Solution Train. He or she helps the ARTs and specialized teams work in alignment with the solution vision and goals.

- Epic Owners: Epic Owners are responsible for defining, prioritizing and analyzing the business impact of Epics on a portfolio basis.

Together, these roles form the backbone of the SAFe framework. They provide the necessary communication, coordination, and alignment at all levels to ensure that the agile approach is successfully implemented in an organization of any size.

Chapter 3: Agile Release Train - Introduction

Welcome to Chapter 3, where we explore the exciting world of Agile Release Trains (ART). Agile Release Trains represent the heart of the Scaled Agile Framework (SAFe) and have the potential to fundamentally change the way organizations deliver projects and deliver value.

An Agile Release Train is, simply put, a large work unit focused on long-term goals and consisting of several smaller teams. These teams work synchronously on the same goals, oriented around a common Program Increment (PI) schedule. A PI is generally a period of 8 to 12 weeks in which a defined amount of work is completed.

The beauty of the ART concept lies in its ability to enable agility at scale while leveraging the benefits of lean principles and practices. By working together in an ART, organizations can achieve a high level of alignment and alignment while being able to respond quickly to change and deliver continuous value.

However, implementing an ART is no small task. It requires a deep understanding of agile principles and practices, as well as an organizational commitment to culture change. Successful implementation often requires careful planning, clear communication of expectations, and a high level of commitment at all levels of the organization.

In this chapter, we will take a closer look at the structure and dynamics of an ART. We will discuss the key roles within an ART as well as the core processes and procedures that enable everything to run smoothly. In addition, we will look at how an ART fosters collaboration, mitigates risk, and enables a steady flow of value-added supplies.

The Agile Release Train has the potential to be a powerful force for change in your organization. So, hop on board and prepare for an exciting journey as we dive into the depths of ART.

Definition of Agile Release Train

The Agile Release Train (ART) is a central concept in the SAFe framework. It is the primary means of delivering value and represents a long-term organizational unit focused on value. An ART is essentially a large group of agile teams working synchronously to achieve common goals.

An ART typically consists of 50 to 125 people organized into 5 to 12 agile teams. Each of these teams consists of cross-functional members who have the expertise necessary to deliver full-featured, customer-facing features and components. The ART is the primary carrier of business value in SAFe, as it provides the capabilities to build, deploy, and release software in regular, predictable cycles.

An important aspect of ART is its regularity and reliability, similar to a train that departs on time and reaches its destination. The principle of the ART is that it departs at set times - called Program Increments (PIs). A PI is a period of time during which an ART develops and delivers a set of features. A typical PI consists of 4-6 iterations (also known as sprints) and typically lasts eight to twelve weeks.

The Agile Release Train is used to synchronize and align the efforts of many teams towards common goals. With its fixed structure, schedule, and cycles, the ART provides a stable, reliable way to deliver value in large, complex projects and organizations.

Importance of the Agile Release Train in SAFe

THE SAFE PRACTICE GUIDE: AGILE TRANSFORMATION USING THE AGILE RELEASE TRAIN

The Agile Release Train (ART) is at the heart of SAFe and its role is critical to the success of agile transformation in larger organizations. It represents a virtual organization committed to delivering a continuous flow of valuable, finished features to customers.

The importance of ART in SAFe manifests itself in several ways:

- Synchronization: The ART puts different teams on a common path of synchronization and collaboration. It harmonizes iterations and program increments so that all teams work in a unified, predictable rhythm. This synchronicity facilitates planning, coordination, and integration of work across multiple teams.

- Delivery of Value: The ART focuses on the delivery of business value. He is responsible for the development, integration, testing and delivery of complete features that can be used immediately.

- Program Increments (PIs): By defining PIs, the ART delivers at specified intervals. Each PI delivers identifiable business value and helps make progress visible and shorten feedback loops.

- Alignment: The ART provides common understanding and alignment among teams. Through joint PI planning events, inspection, and alignment, the ART can ensure that all teams are headed in the same direction and have the same goals.

- Innovation and learning: An important feature of the ART is to foster a culture of innovation and continuous learning. The regular inclusion of innovation and learning cycles in each PI promotes continuous improvement and adaptability.

The Agile Release Train is thus not only a mechanism for coordinating work and delivering value, but also serves as a catalyst for culture change toward greater agility, collaboration, and customer focus.

Comparison of ART with traditional approaches

The Agile Release Train (ART) represents a paradigm shift when compared to traditional approaches to project management and software development.

1. Rhythm and predictability: Traditional methods often operate with individual projects that are planned and executed independently. In contrast, ART operates with a predictable, fixed rhythm - program increments (PIs) - that allow teams to focus on the continuous flow of work, rather than project-based deadlines.
2. Flexibility versus rigid planning: In the traditional waterfall model, much of the planning is done in advance, leaving little room for change once the project has begun. ART, on the other hand, emphasizes adaptability and continuous improvement. The plan for each PI is created collaboratively and provides room for changes and adjustments based on feedback and learning from previous PIs.
3. Collaboration versus silos: Traditional methods tend to organize work in silos, with each team or department working on its own tasks in isolation. In ART, however, teams work closely together, coordinating their work and sharing responsibility for the end result. This fosters a high level of collaboration and transparency.
4. Value creation versus task completion: Unlike traditional approaches, which often focus on the completion of individual

tasks, ART focuses on the continuous delivery of customer value. Prioritization of work is based on business value and teams are accountable for delivering finished, usable features, not just completed tasks.

In summary, the Agile Release Train represents a flexible, adaptive, and collaborative approach to work that is strongly focused on the flow of customer value and continuous improvement. This is a stark contrast to the more rigid, more task-focused, and often siloed approaches of traditional methodologies.

Roles within the ART

The Agile Release Train (ART) includes several roles that interact with each other to ensure the continuous flow of value. At the core of this unique structure are the following key roles:

- Release Train Engineer (RTE): As the "Scrum Master of the Train", the RTE is responsible for coordinating the entire train. This role monitors and manages the flow of work, resolves blockages, communicates with stakeholders, and organizes and facilitates the planning and review meetings of the program increments.

- Product Management: the role of Product Management is to define the vision and roadmap for the product and set priorities for the backlog. They work closely with the teams and stakeholders to ensure that the work being done on the ART delivers the greatest possible business value.

- System Architect/Engineer: The System Architect is responsible for the technical integrity of the overall product. They define the architecture, technical standards, and guidelines and ensure that teams work within those guidelines.

- Business Owners: The Business Owners are key players with a strong stake in the outcomes of the ART. They have a vested interest in value creation and are heavily involved in decision making and prioritization of backlog items.

- Agile Teams: At the fundamental level of ART are the Agile Teams, which are composed of cross-functional members, including the role of Scrum Master, Product Owner, and team members. These teams are self-organized and responsible for completing the work in each PI.

Each of these roles plays a critical role in the successful operation of the Agile Release Train. Together, they work to ensure coordinated and effective delivery of value while upholding Agile principles of self-organization and continuous improvement.

Responsibilities within the ART

Now that we've introduced the roles within the Agile Release Train (ART), it's time to dive deeper into their respective responsibilities.

Release Train Engineer (RTE): As the primary "train driver," the RTE is responsible for ensuring the smooth operation of the ART. This includes removing obstacles, facilitating communication between teams and stakeholders, and ensuring that work on the train is done in accordance with SAFe principles and practices.

2. product management: this role is the driving force behind the product, responsible for defining and communicating the product vision, prioritizing the program backlog, and working with stakeholders and teams to ensure that the work delivered on the ART delivers maximum value.

System Architect/Engineer: The System Architect is the technical guardian of the ART. He or she defines the system architecture and technical guidelines and ensures that the development teams adhere to them. They work closely with product management to ensure that the technical and product vision are aligned.

4. business owners: The responsibility of the business owners lies in strategic alignment. They are the key stakeholders of the ART and have direct influence on prioritization of work and decision making to ensure that the ART delivers the correct value streams.

5. Agile Teams: Each team in ART consists of a group of professionals who work closely together to ensure incremental value delivery. They are responsible for delivering high quality, fully tested work packages that meet the requirements of the product owners.

Although each of these roles has specific responsibilities, the success of the ART is based on a culture of collaboration and self-organization. Each role is critical to ensuring a continuous flow of value delivery and works closely with the other roles to achieve this.

Chapter 4: Agile Release Train - Roles and Responsibilities

In this chapter, we look at the different roles and responsibilities found in an Agile Release Train (ART). ARTs are entities composed of multiple teams that work together with a common vision and a clear purpose. In this context, clearly defined roles and responsibilities are critical to the effectiveness and efficiency of an ART.

There are several key roles in an ART, including the Scrum Master, the Product Owner, the Architect, and the Business Owner.

The Scrum Master is an important facilitator and coach within the team. He ensures that the team uses the Scrum process effectively and creates a working environment in which the team can develop its full potential. The Scrum Master acts as a champion of agility and is constantly working to remove obstacles that may prevent the team from doing its job.

The Product Owner has the central task of communicating the vision and strategy of the product and managing the priorities of the product backlog. He makes important decisions about product development and ensures that the team is always focused on the most value-adding features.

The Architect is responsible for the technical direction and architecture of the product. This role involves making design decisions, technology choices, and implementing best practices to ensure the quality and consistency of the product.

The Business Owner, on the other hand, represents the interests of the stakeholders and the company within the ART. He works closely with the product owner to ensure that the product vision and strategy are in line with the business goals.

All of these roles work hand-in-hand to create a synergy that enables value to be delivered in an efficient and effective manner. Each role brings a specific expertise and perspective that helps guide the ART on its path to continuous improvement and world-class results. An effective ART requires a high level of collaboration, communication, and respect for the individual skills and responsibilities that each role brings.

Release Train Engineer - Role and Responsibilities

At the heart of the Agile Release Train (ART) is the role of the Release Train Engineer (RTE). The RTE is an integral part of the ART, effectively its engineer, keeping the train on the tracks and ensuring that it arrives at its destination on schedule.

The role of the RTE is multi-layered and encompasses a variety of responsibilities, many of which involve working with other teams and members of the ART. In this section, we will take a closer look at some of the key responsibilities of the RTE:

1. coordination and governance of the ART: The RTE is responsible for organizing and conducting Program Increment (PI) planning meetings and other key meetings. He/she leads program management and assists in resolving issues and interdependencies between teams.

2. remove obstacles: During the development process, obstacles may always arise that impede progress. It is the responsibility of the RTE to identify these obstacles and find ways to remove them to ensure trouble-free operation.

3. ensure compliance with SAFe principles: As a key member of the ART, the RTE must ensure that work is performed in accordance with SAFe principles and practices. He/she promotes a culture of agility and continuous improvement within the platoon.

4. supporting the teams: An essential aspect of the RTE's role is to support the teams within the ART. He or she acts as a coach, supports team members, helps resolve conflicts, and promotes collaboration and communication.

5. reporting and communication: Finally, the RTE plays a crucial role in communication, both within the ART and externally. He or she is responsible for reporting the ART's progress to stakeholders and ensuring that all members of the platoon are aware of relevant information and decisions.

It is important to note that the role of the RTE, although focused on leadership and governance, is not hierarchical. Rather, the RTE is a servant-leader who focuses on the well-being of the ART and its members.

Product Owner - Role and Responsibilities

In the world of the Scaled Agile Framework (SAFe), the Product Owner (PO) is a central figure who acts as a liaison between the development team and the stakeholders. This role brings with it numerous responsibilities aimed at ensuring that product development runs effectively and efficiently while meeting stakeholder expectations.

Let's start with a deeper look at some of the core responsibilities that the PO bears:

1. management of the product backlog: One of the main responsibilities of the PO is to manage the product backlog. This includes prioritizing requirements and ensuring that development work is in line with business goals and customer needs.

2. work with stakeholders: As the liaison between the team and stakeholders, the PO is responsible for ensuring that communication flows smoothly. She or he should understand the stakeholders' requirements and translate them into clear instructions and priorities for the development team.

3. establish acceptance criteria: The PO works closely with the development team to ensure that requirements are clearly understood. A key aspect of this is defining acceptance criteria for each requirement to ensure that the delivered product meets expectations.

4. participation in planning and review meetings: The PO plays an active role in various SAFe events, including Program Increment (PI) planning and review meetings. Here, the PO ensures that the team's goals and priorities are in alignment with stakeholder expectations.

5. acceptance of the finished product: as the representative of the customers and users, it is the PO's task to check and accept the finished product. She or he ensures that the delivered results meet the defined requirements and provide the expected benefits.

Each of these responsibilities is designed to maintain a balance between the needs of the stakeholders and the capabilities of the development team. The PO thus bears an enormous responsibility, but at the same time contributes significantly to the success of the ART.

Architect - role and responsibilities

The architect plays a critical role in the Scaled Agile Framework (SAFe). In the complex landscape of agile software development, the architect acts as a visionary leader and technical guru, helping to shape and guide the Agile Release Train (ART) technology strategy.

Let's take a closer look at the architect's key responsibilities in a SAFe environment:

1. technological vision: the elaboration of a technological vision that is in line with the company's objectives is a central task of the architect. She or he should be able to create a long-term plan for technological development that takes into account both current and future requirements.

2. design and maintain system architecture: The architect is responsible for designing and maintaining the system architecture. This includes selecting appropriate technologies and architectural models to achieve business goals and meet quality standards.

3. evaluate technical risks: it is the architect's task to identify and evaluate technical risks. She or he must propose solutions to minimize these risks and ensure the robustness and performance of the system.

4. making technical decisions: In the SAFe context, the architect also makes important technical decisions, for example, regarding the selection of technologies, the design of components, or the implementation of security standards. These decisions should always be based on business goals and stakeholder needs.

5. collaboration with other roles: The architect works closely with other key roles such as product owner, release train engineer, and development teams. Effective collaboration is critical to ensure that technical solutions meet requirements and contribute to achieving business goals.

Overall, the role of the architect in the SAFe model is significant. She or he occupies a position that requires strategic thinking, technical expertise, and effective communication to lay the technical foundation on which the Agile Release Train can successfully ride.

Business Owner - Role and Responsibilities

In the SAFe environment, the role of the Business Owner involves much more than mere ownership. As a key player in the design and implementation of the Agile Release Train (ART), the Business Owner represents the business interests and is the bridge between the business side and the technical teams.

Let's take a look at the key responsibilities of a business owner in the SAFe environment:

1. decision maker and prioritizer: A business owner makes strategic decisions regarding the product or service portfolio. He is responsible for prioritizing requirements based on business objectives and market conditions.

2. stakeholder management: The business owner is the link between the various stakeholders, including customers, product teams and company management. She or he is responsible for communicating and managing expectations on all sides.

3. take responsibility for value creation: the business owner is instrumental in maximizing business value. He should oversee the implementation of measures aimed at improving productivity, quality and customer satisfaction.

4. collaboration with product management: the business owner works closely with product management to ensure that the product vision and strategy are in line with business objectives and are successfully implemented.

5. participation in inspection and customization events: As a member of the ART, the Business Owner actively participates in key events such as PI planning meetings and system demos. In doing so, she or he provides feedback and initiates necessary corrective actions.

In summary, the Business Owner is a central figure in the SAFe landscape. With one foot in the business world and the other in the technical environment, the Business Owner brings a perspective that aligns both business objectives and technical implementation. By filling this gap, the Business Owner enables effective and value-creating implementation of SAFe principles and practices.

Cooperation of the roles

Collaboration between the different roles in an Agile Release Train (ART) is essential to the success of any SAFe project. Effective collaboration allows the different teams to leverage their individual skills and expertise to achieve common goals and ultimately generate more value for the business.

Let's start with the relationship between the Release Train Engineer (RTE) and the Product Owner (PO). The RTE acts as the servant leader for the entire Agile Release Train, while the PO represents and prioritizes stakeholder requirements. Together, they ensure that the right requirements are addressed in the right order and that the work is in alignment with business goals. They make product development decisions and share their vision and priorities with the team.

The architect also plays a critical role in the collaboration. He works closely with the PO and RTE to ensure that the technical implementation of the requirements is in line with the product vision and business goals. He also conducts technical discussions and supports the team in overcoming technical challenges.

The business owner is another important role in this equation. She or he works closely with the PO and RTE to ensure that the company's business goals are reflected in product development. The Business Owner acts as the voice of the company and helps keep the focus on the business value of the work.

This collaboration between the different roles requires open communication, transparency and respect for each team member's respective skills and responsibilities. In a well-coordinated ART, everyone works together to overcome obstacles, create value and drive continuous improvement. In doing so, each individual is committed to not losing sight of the common goal: delivering high-quality products or services that maximize business value.

Chapter 5: Agile Release Train - Processes

This chapter is dedicated to the specific processes implemented and applied within an Agile Release Train (ART). The ART is more than just a collection of teams; it also embodies a robust infrastructure of processes that help structure and optimize the way it works. These processes are not rigid prescriptions, but flexible enough to adapt to different contexts and challenges. They represent best practices based on the principles of agility and serve to embed them in daily work.

One of the core elements of these processes is Program Increment (PI) planning, which we have already explained in detail in a separate section. PI planning is a multi-day workshop that sets the pace and direction of ART and ensures that all teams are working toward a common goal.

Another central process within the ART is the Iteration Review. At this regular meeting, each team presents the progress it has made and discusses any problems or challenges. This gives the teams the opportunity to receive feedback and continuously improve their work.

Risk management is also an essential process at ART. At regular intervals, the teams identify and evaluate risks and formulate measures to counter them. This can be done at team or program level, depending on the size and scope of the risk.

In addition, dependency management is an important process. Because work in an ART is typically highly interconnected, it is critical to identify and manage dependencies between teams and their tasks. This can help avoid delays and ensure that work flows smoothly.

Finally, the retrospective also plays a central role in the processes of the ART. This is a regular meeting in which teams reflect on their work and identify opportunities for improvement. The insights gained from these meetings are directly incorporated into the planning and execution of future tasks.

Overall, these processes form the backbone of ART and enable teams to work together effectively and efficiently. They help teams respond to change, achieve continuous improvement, and create a constant flow of value. By embedding them in the principles of agility, they help teams to successfully master the challenges of the modern software development process.

PI planning - description and meaning

PI planning, short for Program Increment Planning, is a central process in the application of SAFe and one of the prominent procedures within an Agile Release Train (ART). It is a recurring, collaborative planning event that enables all members of the ART to come together and is the heart of the SAFe framework.

But what exactly is PI planning? At its core, it is a two-day workshop that enables teams to plan work for the next Program Increment, typically for a period of 8 to 12 weeks. This is where all participants, including stakeholders, meet to jointly plan and agree on the goals and workload for the upcoming quarter.

The planning process involves a number of activities: Alignment with business goals, synchronization between teams, establishment of team and program PI goals, identification of risks and dependencies, and ultimately confirmation and commitment to a common plan. Here, the Release Train Engineer plays an important role as facilitator and moderator.

The importance of PI planning in the SAFe framework cannot be overstated. It creates transparency and promotes alignment between teams, leading to better coordination, faster feedback, and ultimately higher product quality. PI planning helps identify risks early and initiate actions to mitigate them. It ensures that all teams are aligned on the same goals and fosters a culture of open communication and collaboration. In short, PI planning is the binder that holds the ART together and generates maximum business value.

Workflows within the ART

In the SAFe framework, the consistent and reliable "ticking" of the Agile Release Train (ART) is enabled by well-defined workflows. These workflows provide a structured pattern for executing and coordinating work. They create clarity and certainty of expectations, which helps teams function and collaborate efficiently and effectively.

The general workflow within an ART is cyclical and sequential. It all starts with the aforementioned PI planning, where the vision and goals for the next Program Increment are set. Following PI planning, the execution cycle begins. This consists of several iterations, typically four to six, during which teams work to achieve their PI goals. Each iteration typically lasts two weeks and includes planning, execution, review, and adjustment.

Within each iteration, teams follow an iterative and incremental development approach based on the Scrum or Kanban framework. They take user stories from their backlog and work to turn them into functional software. During this time, daily standup meetings are held to review progress and identify any roadblocks or issues.

At the end of each iteration, an iteration review and retrospective takes place. This involves assessing the value delivered and reflecting on how collaboration and processes can be improved. At the end of the Program Increment, an Inspect-and-Adapt workshop is held to summarize ART-level learning and determine improvements for the next PI cycle.

It is this structured but flexible way of working that makes the ART effective, responsive and enables the continuous delivery of value. It builds trust, fosters collaboration, and enables continuous learning and improvement. Thus, the flow of work within an ART is a key component for success in the SAFe framework.

Detailed description of the work processes

A detailed analysis of the workflows within an Agile Release Train (ART) helps to better understand the interrelationships and dependencies within the individual process steps. As previously mentioned, each cycle starts with PI planning, followed by several iterations, and concludes with an Inspect-and-Adapt workshop.

PI planning is a two-day event attended by all ART members. The goal of this event is to define a shared vision and goals for the next Program Increment (PI) and create a plan for achieving them. The plan is visualized in the form of a "PI Planning Board" that shows the planned work elements for each iteration and team. It is also a time for risk assessment and mitigation, as well as alignment and coordination between teams.

Following PI planning, the iterations in which the teams execute their work begin. Each iteration usually lasts two weeks and includes several process steps:

- The Iteration Planning Meeting at the beginning of each iteration, where the team selects the user stories from the backlog that they will work on in the upcoming iteration.

- The daily standup meetings where each team member reports what they have done since the last meeting, what they will do between now and the next meeting, and if they have encountered any obstacles.

- The Iteration Review, in which the team presents the work completed in the iteration to stakeholders and solicits feedback.

- The retrospective, in which the team reflects on its collaboration and processes and identifies opportunities for improvement.

At the end of the PI cycle, an Inspect and Adapt workshop is held. The purpose of this workshop is to evaluate the results of the completed Program Increment, summarize learning experiences, and determine improvements for the next PI cycle.

Through this clear structure and methodical approach, the flow of work within an ART forms the backbone for the continuous improvement process and continuous value creation. It is a balance between planning and flexibility, between individual and collective work, that is the secret of success of the Agile Release Train.

Risk management in ART

Risk management is a central task in any ART, as risks can impact the teams' ability to deliver value. In the context of SAFe and ART, risk management is viewed as a continuous, integral part of the entire process, not an isolated task performed only at specific points in time.

One aspect of risk management in ART is risk analysis. In this analysis, potential risks are identified and assessed. The assessment includes determining the likelihood of the risk occurring and the impact if the risk does occur. Actions are developed to mitigate, transfer, avoid, or accept each risk, depending on which strategy is most appropriate.

Another aspect is risk communication. Information about risks and measures to mitigate them are communicated to all relevant stakeholders. This communication can take various forms, such as status reports, meetings, or dashboards.

Risk control is the third essential aspect of risk management in ART. Here, the implemented measures are monitored to ensure that they are effective and reduce the risk to an acceptable level. If the measures are not effective, they are adjusted or replaced by others.

A special part of risk management in ART is ROAMing of risks (Resolved, Owned, Accepted, Mitigated). This method is used as part of PI planning and makes it possible to make risks visible, evaluate them, and assign them a responsible person who will ensure that the risk is mitigated or resolved.

Finally, learning from mistakes is also part of risk management. Errors and problems that have occurred are analyzed and viewed as learning opportunities. By understanding the causes, similar problems can be avoided in the future.

Risk management in ART is a shared responsibility: everyone in the platoon contributes to identifying, assessing and mitigating risks. As such, it is an essential part of ensuring the success of ARTs and ensuring the continuous flow of value.

Dependency management in ART

Dependency management is a critical component in an Agile Release Train because in today's complex working world, almost all projects and processes are interdependent in some way. Dependencies can exist within an ART (i.e., between teams), between different ARTs, or between an ART and external entities.

One of the first tasks in dependency management is to identify all relevant dependencies. In SAFe, this is done during the PI planning session, where each team maps its dependencies to other teams and visualizes them on the program board.

The next step is to prioritize these dependencies. This can be done on the basis of various criteria, such as the risk posed by the dependency or the importance of the dependency for the overall process.

Coordination is another important aspect of dependency management. It refers to the measures taken to ensure that all teams and individuals affected by a dependency have the information and resources they need at the right time. This can be achieved, for example, through regular coordination meetings, status updates, or even special tools and platforms to support collaboration.

In the ART, there is also a special role, the RTE (Release Train Engineer), who is responsible, among other things, for monitoring and coordinating dependency management. He ensures that all dependencies are correctly identified and appropriately managed.

A final important aspect of dependency management is the monitoring and control of dependencies. This involves continuously reviewing how dependencies are handled and adjusting them if necessary.

Effective dependency management enables ARTs to ensure smooth execution of their activities, effectively manage interdependencies, and thus minimize the risks associated with these dependencies. This helps improve productivity and efficiency and ensures that value is delivered continuously and reliably.

Chapter 6: Agile Release Train - Activities and Methods

In this chapter, we will take a closer look at the specific activities and methods used within an Agile Release Train (ART). An ART is not only a grouping of teams, but also a set of processes and activities designed to ensure a smooth flow of work and enable continuous value creation.

One of the central activities within the ART is PI planning, which we have already discussed in detail in Chapter 5. In this process, which lasts several days, all teams of the ART plan the next Program Increment (PI) together. Through this meeting, dependencies can be identified, priorities can be set, and the entire train can be focused on a common goal.

Another key process is the Daily Stand-Up. This is a short, usually 15-minute meeting held daily where each team member briefly reports on their work, any issues they are facing, and the plan for the day ahead. This promotes communication within the team and helps to quickly identify and eliminate obstacles.

The System Demo is another important activity within the ART. During a System Demo, each team presents its results achieved in the last iteration to the rest of the ART and stakeholders. This allows for a review of progress and early feedback that can contribute to further improvement.

Finally, retrospectives are also a central part of the work process in an ART. In these sessions, the teams look back on the past iteration and reflect on what went well and what could be improved. The results of these retrospectives are incorporated into the planning of the next iteration and thus contribute to continuous improvement.

All these activities and methods are closely linked and contribute to the ART's ability to function as a unit. They enable the teams to work synchronously, support each other, and deliver a continuous value stream together. They ensure that the ART can respond flexibly to change without losing sight of the overall goals. And they help make the principles and values of agility a reality in day-to-day work.

Coordination activities in the Agile Release Train (ART)

The coordination of activities in an Agile Release Train (ART) is a central aspect of SAFe. This is about synchronizing the collective efforts of teams and stakeholders to achieve common goals.

At their core, coordination activities are systemic actions that ensure the entire train system runs efficiently and effectively. These activities encompass a variety of tasks ranging from synchronizing iterations and program increments to managing dependencies and coordinating delivery and release.

A key aspect of coordination activities is the synchronization of iterations. In SAFe, all teams within an ART work in the same iterations to ensure consistent delivery of value. Synchronization of iterations ensures that all teams are working in sync and their work is aligned. This concurrency promotes a common goal orientation and improves coordination between teams.

Another important area of coordination activities is the management of dependencies. In any ART, there are dependencies between teams and between teams and other parts of the organization. These dependencies need to be actively managed to minimize risk and ensure that all teams are able to do their work effectively. In SAFe, this is achieved through specific roles and meetings, such as the Scrum of Scrums and the Release Train Engineer.

Finally, delivery and release coordination is central to the coordination activities. In SAFe, the concept of continuous delivery is used to ensure that value is continuously delivered to customers. Delivery and release coordination ensures that the work of all teams in the organization comes together effectively to ensure consistent and high-quality delivery of value.

In summary, coordination activities in an ART are essential requirements to ensure that the work of all teams and stakeholders is effectively aligned. Through effective coordination, organizations can ensure that they continuously deliver value to their customers and achieve their goals.

Communication activities in the Agile Release Train (ART)

Communication in the Agile Release Train (ART) is an indispensable element to ensure the smooth functioning of the entire system. The importance of effective and constant communication cannot be overemphasized, as it is the lifeblood of a successful ART. Within the ART, there are specific communication activities designed to disseminate information, address issues, and promote collaboration.

A basic communication activity is the daily stand-up meeting or Daily Scrum. It is a short, time-limited meeting that helps teams stay up to date and address any obstacles. Each team member shares what he or she has accomplished since the last stand-up, what he or she wants to accomplish today, and if there are any obstacles that might hinder his or her work.

Another important communication channel is the Scrum of Scrums. It is a coordination meeting for Scrum teams that serves to facilitate the flow of information between the teams. The Scrum of Scrums builds on the information developed in the Daily Scrum and makes it possible to improve collaboration between teams by passing on important information at ART level.

For a higher level of communication, there is the ART Synchronization Meeting, often referred to as ART Sync. This meeting allows for effective communication of information and decisions that affect the entire ART. It is a regular meeting led by the Release Train Engineer (RTE) and can be attended by executives, Product Owners, Scrum Masters, and other stakeholders.

Another communication mechanism is the Inspect & Adapt (I&A) session that occurs at the end of each Program Increment (PI). It is an opportunity for the entire ART to reflect on the work of the past increment and identify areas for improvement.

These communication activities are essential to ensure that all teams in the ART are on the same page, that information flows effectively, and that issues and challenges are addressed and resolved quickly. They foster a culture of open communication, which is essential for Agile and SAFe to succeed.

Use of Scrum in the Agile Release Train (ART)

Scrum, an agile framework characterized by its adaptability and efficiency, plays a central role in the structure of the Agile Release Train (ART). Scrum provides teams within the ART with a method to organize their work while promoting transparency, inspection, and adaptation.

In an ART, team members are divided into smaller, cross-functional Scrum teams. Each of these teams usually consists of five to nine members and includes roles such as the product owner, the scrum master, and the team members who do the actual work.

A key feature of Scrum is the sprint or iteration model. Sprints are time-limited work periods in which a specific set of tasks is to be completed. Within an ART, Scrum teams usually follow the same sprint timeframe to facilitate coordination and planning.

The product owner plays a central role in the Scrum model. He or she is responsible for maintaining the product backlog, a prioritized list of features, changes, and fixes needed for a product. The product owner makes decisions about which tasks to include in the next sprint based on business value and priority.

A key event in Scrum is the daily stand-up meeting, or Daily Scrum, in which each team member briefly describes what they have done since the last meeting, what they will do today, and if they are encountering any obstacles. This fosters a culture of transparency and allows the team to quickly focus on problems and find solutions.

Implementing Scrum in an ART provides a number of benefits, including improved communication, increased transparency, and the ability to respond quickly to change. This helps teams stay focused while having the flexibility to adapt to changing business needs. It ensures that progress is visible and tangible, and that obstacles can be quickly identified and addressed.

Use of Kanban in the Agile Release Train (ART)

Kanban is another method that is often used in an Agile Release Train (ART). Originating from the Japanese Toyota Production System, Kanban is used in Agile software development to visualize and manage the flow of work.

At its core, Kanban is an approach to managing workload in real time, with the goal of optimizing performance, eliminating waste, and promoting continuous improvement. The basic principles of the Kanban approach - visualization, work in progress (WIP) limitation, flow management and continuous improvement - are very useful in an ART.

In an ART, Kanban boards are often used to track the activities within a sprint or iteration. These boards consist of multiple columns that represent the different stages of the work process, such as "To Do," "In Progress," and "Done." Each task or work package is represented on a board, which is then moved from one column to the next depending on which stage of processing it is in.

Limiting work in progress (WIP limit) is another important aspect of Kanban. By limiting the number of tasks being processed at one time, the focus is on completion rather than initiating new tasks. This can help reduce cycle time and improve cycle time.

The principle of flow management is also central to Kanban. It's about monitoring the speed and evenness with which work flows through the system. Through regular reviews and adjustments, a team can improve its work practices and minimize bottlenecks.

Using Kanban in an ART can increase transparency, improve productivity, and help foster a culture of continuous improvement. It enables teams to make their work visible, track their progress, and respond quickly to problems. In doing so, it helps the team focus on common goals and improvements.

Tools to support the Agile Release Train (ART)

In today's digital world, tools are essential to increase the efficiency and effectiveness of workflows. In an Agile Release Train (ART), various tools can be used to facilitate collaboration and communication, increase productivity and monitor progress.

Among the basic tools used in an ART are project management and task tracking tools. These are used to keep track of the various tasks and their progress. Examples of such tools are Jira, Trello or Asana. They allow tasks to be created, assigned, and tracked, and often offer features such as boards, lists, and maps to visualize the work.

Another important tool in an ART is a collaboration tool. This can be a chat tool like Slack or Microsoft Teams, or it can be a more comprehensive collaboration tool like Confluence or Sharepoint that provides document sharing, discussion, and collaborative working capabilities. Such tools foster communication and collaboration within the team and can help bridge information gaps and make collaboration more effective.

In addition, specialized tools can be used for specific aspects of ART. For example, tools can be used to support Scrum or Kanban to help plan and track sprints and visualize the flow of work. Other specialized tools can be used to support activities such as risk assessment, dependency management, or quality control.

It is important to note that the selection of tools should be tailored to the specific requirements and circumstances of the ART and the company. It is also important that the tools are well integrated into the team's workflows and that team members are appropriately trained to use the tools effectively.

Overall, tools play a key role in making processes in an ART efficient and smooth and in promoting collaboration and communication within the team. They are an indispensable tool for optimizing the ART's performance and productivity and fostering a culture of continuous improvement.

Chapter 7: Agile Release Train - Interrelationships and Integration in the Overall System

The effectiveness of the Agile Release Train (ART) is not limited to its internal dynamics and processes. It unfolds its full potential only when it is successfully embedded in the entire ecosystem of a company. It is important to understand that the ART is not an isolated element, but an integral part of the larger whole that interacts with other parts of the enterprise system.

At the outset, it is important to highlight the link between ART and portfolio management. Portfolio management provides strategic direction and prioritization of initiatives at the corporate level. These prioritizations flow into the program increments of ART and influence the work that is done in the individual teams. This creates a bidirectional relationship: while portfolio management provides direction, ART provides continuous feedback on progress and potential obstacles, which in turn informs decision-making at the portfolio level.

The ART is also closely linked to the various corporate functions such as finance, human resources, marketing and sales. These departments must adapt their processes and ways of working to the rhythm and methods of the ART. For example, finance must be able to track and quantify the value stream flowing through the ART to support financial planning and reporting.

Within the IT ecosystem, the ART interacts with various other teams and units. These include, for example, operations teams, which are responsible for the provision and operation of services, and support and helpdesk teams, which handle customer requests. By working closely with and coordinating with these teams, the ART can ensure that the products and services developed can be effectively commissioned and supported.

In addition, the ART also has points of contact with external partners and stakeholders. These may include customers, suppliers, service providers and regulatory authorities. Through active stakeholder management, the ART can ensure that the requirements and expectations of these stakeholders are included in the planning and execution of the work.

In summary, the integration of the ART into the overall system of a company plays a crucial role in its success. It requires consistent alignment and coordination between the ART and the various other elements of the system to ensure that they are all aligned and can work together effectively. Only in this way can the ART develop its full potential and make a maximum contribution to the company's success.

Interactions between ART and other SAFe levels

In the context of SAFe (Scaled Agile Framework), the Agile Release Train (ART) represents the program level. It is the central component that connects the Team and Portfolio levels. Understanding the interactions between these levels is critical to understanding the role and influence of the ART in the overall system.

The team level is the basis of ART. It comprises all agile teams working on a specific value stream. Each team is self-organizing in itself and decides autonomously on its way of working. But within the ART, a common vision and an overarching direction is provided by the higher levels. The ART is thus the link that coordinates and synchronizes the independent work of the teams. It ensures that all teams focus their energies on the common goals and work together to achieve the greater whole.

The portfolio level, on the other hand, provides the strategic framework for the ART. Here, the company's long-term goals and strategic initiatives are defined, which guide the work at the program and team levels. The portfolio level decides which value streams will be funded and where investments will be made. These decisions determine the priorities and direction of the ART. Conversely, the ART informs the portfolio level through regular reports on the progress and results of the work. In this way, adjustments can be made to the strategy and investments if deemed necessary.

Finally, one should not neglect the ART's interactions with the Large Solution level, which sits between the Program and Portfolio levels. In larger organizations where multiple ARTs work together to create large and complex solutions, this level serves to ensure coordination and integration of work across multiple ARTs. The ART must therefore work closely with other trains and the coordination structures at this level.

It is therefore obvious that the ART is a node within the SAFe framework. It absorbs influences from different levels and acts back on them. In order to work effectively, it must therefore understand these interactions and actively shape them. Only in this way can it make its contribution to achieving the overarching corporate goals.

Process of scaling the ART

In organizations where project dimensions and complexity are increasing, scaling Agile Release Train (ART) is inevitable. However, it is not an easy task as it requires precise planning, coordination and implementation to ensure success. The following suggests a basic process that can help in scaling the ART.

The first step is to evaluate the need. In this phase, it is critical to understand the why behind scaling. Is it necessary due to increased project size, more extensive product portfolio, or organizational change? Clarifying these questions helps determine the scope and scale of scaling.

The second step is to analyze the current state of the ART. Which teams are already part of the train and how do they work together? What processes and tools are already being used? A detailed analysis helps to determine the starting point and identify areas that need to be improved or adapted.

The third step is planning for scaling. In this phase, strategic decisions are made. How many new teams should be added? How should these teams be organized and coordinated? What will the new structure of the ART look like? Here, it can be useful to fall back on the concept of the "solution train" if several ARTs are working on a complex solution.

The fourth step is the implementation of scaling. In this phase, the new teams are built and integrated into the expanded ART. This requires effective communication and training to introduce the new teams to the ART's ways of working and to foster collaboration.

The final step is review and adjustment. After scaling has been implemented, it is important to evaluate its success and make any adjustments. It can be helpful to use retrospective meetings to gather feedback and identify opportunities for improvement.

This process should not be understood as a rigid step-by-step guide, but rather as a flexible model that should be adapted to the specific needs and circumstances of the company. Scaling is a complex task that requires a high degree of flexibility, adaptability and continuous improvement.

Examples of successful ART implementations

To make the concept and the effect of the Agile Release Train (ART) tangible, case studies and success stories are an excellent means. They not only provide illustrative material, but also inspiration and suggestions for one's own practice. Three exemplary implementations of ART in different companies are presented below.

The first example is that of an international software company specializing in security software. Prior to the introduction of ART, the company was struggling to efficiently coordinate its numerous globally distributed teams and ensure the interaction of the various components of their software. By introducing an ART that united all teams under one roof, the company was able to increase productivity, reduce the time-to-market of its products, and ensure higher quality software.

The second example concerns a large financial services company. In this context, the company faced the challenge of becoming more agile in a highly regulated and traditional environment. By implementing the

ART concept, the company was able not only to improve its internal processes and collaboration between teams, but also to bring its services to market faster and more efficiently. In addition, the ART helped extend agility to all levels of the company by serving as a model for other departments.

The third example is a telecommunications company that faced the challenge of constantly providing its customers with new and improved services in order to remain competitive in a highly competitive market. By implementing an ART, the company was able to accelerate its development cycles, improve collaboration between teams, and ensure that the services provided were always up to date.

These examples show that implementing an ART can be successful in a variety of contexts and industries. They underscore the versatility of the concept and its ability to improve collaboration, efficiency and quality in companies. It is important to note that the introduction of an ART should always be adapted to the specific needs and circumstances of the company in question.

Chapter 8: Challenges and possible solutions when using the Agile Release Train

An Agile Release Train (ART) undoubtedly brings many benefits - from increased efficiency to better team collaboration. But as with any organizational change, there are challenges to overcome. This chapter presents some of these challenges and offers concrete solutions to facilitate and optimize the transition to an ART.

Challenge 1: Culture change

Agility is more than just a new process - it requires a paradigm shift that is deeply embedded in the corporate culture. Teams must learn to think and act in new, agile ways that are often met with resistance.

Solution approach: For a successful culture change, it is essential that top management stands behind the initiative and actively supports it. Employees need training and education to understand and apply the principles and methods of agility. In addition, the change should take place gradually and with continuous communication and support.

Challenge 2: Scaling

An ART is a complex system that requires effective coordination and management. Scaling agile processes to this level can present challenges, especially in large organizations with many teams.

Solution approach: It is important to have a clear understanding of the structure and functioning of the ART and to ensure that there are sufficient resources and support for scaling. In addition, it can be helpful to start with a pilot project in the initial phase to gain experience and identify potential barriers.

Challenge 3: Coordination between teams

Many teams work together in an ART, which can make coordination and communication complex. Misunderstandings and conflicts can affect productivity.

Solution approach: Regular meetings and exchange formats, such as PI planning, are critical to keep everyone on the same page. Equally important is a strong Scrum Master Team that serves as a communication bridge between the teams.

Overall, implementing an ART requires patience, commitment, and constant adaptation. However, with the right planning and support, it can become a powerful tool for enterprise-level agility.

Common difficulties in the implementation of ART

Implementing an Agile Release Train (ART) can present a variety of difficulties. It is important to be aware of them and prepare for them to ensure a smooth implementation. Here are some of the most common challenges organizations encounter when implementing ART:

Lack of understanding of agile: Teams often lack a deep understanding of the agile principles and practices that underpin ART. This can lead to teams having difficulty adapting their ways of working and recognizing the value of agile.

Inadequate training and support: ART requires specific knowledge and skills. Without sufficient training and support, it can be difficult to learn and use these new methods effectively.

Resistance to change: As with any major change, there may be resistance to the introduction of ART. Employees may resist the new way of working, especially if it challenges their previous way of working.

Corporate structure: In some cases, the existing corporate structure may conflict with the implementation of ART. For example, a highly hierarchical system may hinder the collaboration and rapid decision-making required in an ART.

Coordination and communication: An ART consists of many teams that need to work together. Coordinating these teams and communicating between them can be a major challenge.

In summary, implementing ART is not without its challenges. Nevertheless, with proper planning, training and support, these difficulties can be overcome and effective, productive ART can be achieved.

Solution strategies for the identified challenges

To overcome the challenges of implementing Agile Release Trains (ART), several solution strategies are applicable. Here are some potential approaches:

Promote agile understanding: It is important that all stakeholders develop a solid understanding of agile principles and practices. This can be achieved through formal training, workshops or continuous learning opportunities.

Investment in training and support: Teams need to be adequately prepared for the new practices and techniques of ART. Investing in training, such as SAFe certification courses, can be helpful here. Coaching and mentoring can also help support teams during the transition.

Change management strategies: Resistance to change can be reduced through effective change management strategies. This can include involving employees in the change process, communicating the benefits of change, and offering support during the transition.

Adapting the corporate structure: In some cases, it may be necessary to rethink and adapt the existing corporate structure to enable the implementation of ART. This could include, for example, promoting flatter hierarchies and strengthening team autonomy.

Promoting coordination and communication: The implementation of ART can be facilitated by introducing tools and practices that promote coordination and communication between teams. This can be achieved, for example, by using agile project management tools and conducting regular stand-ups and retrospectives.

By applying these strategies, organizations can overcome the challenges associated with implementing ART and reap the full benefits of Agile and SAFe.

Role of change management in the use of ART

Change management is a critical factor when using Agile Release Trains (ART). In the Agile world, change is seen as constant and the ability to deal with it effectively is a critical factor for success.

In a company planning to implement ART, change management plays an important role in reducing resistance to change and preparing employees for the new ways of working. It helps to ensure an orderly transition from traditional ways of working to agile methods.

Effective change management involves several aspects:

- Communication: Change management must ensure that all stakeholders are informed about the upcoming changes and the benefits they will bring. Clear and regular communication can help reduce uncertainty and increase acceptance of the change.

- Training: The introduction of ART often requires new skills and knowledge from employees. Change management must ensure that all stakeholders receive the necessary training and support to deal with the new ways of working.

- Support: Change can be unsettling and cause resistance. Change management must therefore provide support to address concerns and help employees adapt to the new methods.

- Measurement and adjustment: Change management must also be able to measure the progress of the change process and make adjustments when necessary. This can be achieved through regular feedback rounds and performance evaluations.

Overall, change management has the task of facilitating the transition to ART and helping to establish an agile culture throughout the company. Without effective change management, the benefits of ART cannot be fully realized.

Organizational development in the context of ART

The implementation of the Agile Release Train (ART) has a significant impact on the organizational structure and culture and is thus an essential component of organizational development. It is a proactive approach that aims to continuously improve and adapt the organization to changing conditions.

In the context of ART, organizational development plays a key role in shaping and promoting an agile corporate culture. It is not just about introducing agile practices, but rather about changing the basic attitudes and behaviors throughout the organization.

In order to successfully implement and use the Agile Release Train, several aspects of organizational development are important:

Leadership: In an agile organization, leadership plays a different role than in traditional structures. Leaders must internalize the principle of "leadership through service" and learn to empower and support teams instead of controlling them.

Structure: Implementing ART may mean adapting the organizational structure to support agile working. This could include breaking down silos and encouraging cross-team collaboration.

Learning and development: An agile organization is a learning organization. It is important to foster continuous learning and improvement to sustain and enhance agility.

Feedback and adaptation: The ability to give and receive feedback and to adapt based on that feedback is critical to ART's success. It is important to establish a culture of open communication and constructive feedback.

Employee engagement: Employees who feel engaged and valued are more likely to accept change and actively participate in the implementation of ART. It is important that employees are seen and treated as key drivers of change.

Organizational development in the context of ART is therefore a comprehensive process involving both structural and cultural changes throughout the organization. It is an ongoing process that requires constant adaptation and improvement.

Chapter 9: Conclusion and outlook

The Agile Release Train (ART) is an impressive model for scaling agile principles and practices at the program and portfolio solution level. It offers the opportunity to transform both teams and organizations and lead them on a successful journey towards greater agility.

The concept of ART ensures that teams in a large organization work toward a common goal. It creates an environment where innovation and collaboration can flourish to bring high-quality products or services to market faster. But as we have seen, introducing and implementing ART is not trivial. It requires profound organizational change and requires continuous commitment and adaptation.

Challenges such as an ingrained silo mentality, resistance to change, and the need to restructure the organization can make ART difficult to implement. But with the right strategies and tools, from clear communication of the change to change management and organizational development, these hurdles can be overcome.

One thing is clear: ART is not a panacea that can be applied to every organization. It requires a conscious decision and is only one of many tools that can support an organization on its path to agility. Therefore, it is important to question oneself again and again and to remain open for adjustments and improvements.

Looking ahead, we see interest in ART and other agile scaling methods remaining strong. As digital transformation continues, more and more companies will recognize the value of an agile approach. At the same time, the environment will continue to evolve, and new challenges and opportunities will emerge. For example, the growing importance of artificial intelligence and automation could provide new opportunities for the further development of ART and agile methods in general.

In the final outlook, it can be said that the Agile Release Train is a valuable tool for scaling agility, but one that requires a willingness to continuously adapt and improve. The journey to full agility is a long-term commitment and ART is just one part of this exciting journey. Future developments in this area will undoubtedly be exciting and innovative, and we look forward to watching and following them.

Summary of the main points

The previous chapters have dealt extensively with the Agile Release Train (ART) as a means of scaling agility in large organizations. Let us summarize here the key points we have covered so far.

First, we have found ART to be an effective method for implementing Lean and Agile principles at the program and portfolio solution level. With its focus on value streams, embedding in the Scaled Agile Framework (SAFe), and building on Agile teams, ART provides a solid foundation for successful scaling.

Second, we highlighted the importance of the various roles within an ART and how they work together to ensure the success of the train. From Release Train Engineers to Product Owners to Team Members, each role contributes in its own way to the achievement of the common goals.

Third, we explored how tools such as Scrum, Kanban, and various software tools help to make ART efficient and effective. These methods and tools enable teams to coordinate their work, overcome obstacles, and continuously improve.

Fourth, we looked at the interactions between the ART and the other layers of the SAFe model. The ART is not an isolated move, but is firmly embedded in the entire system and helps to optimize the flow of value across team boundaries.

Finally, we have addressed the challenges that can arise when introducing and implementing an ART and have presented viable solution strategies for them. Whether it is organizational resistance, structural barriers, or the need for change management, we have discussed how these challenges can be addressed to successfully scale agility.

Future of ART and SAFe

The agile journey has just begun. ART and the SAFe framework have proven to be powerful tools to support this journey, but the world of agile is dynamic and constantly changing. So let's look at what the future might hold for ART and SAFe.

First, the use of ART and SAFe is expected to continue to grow as more organizations realize and seek to implement the benefits of scaling agility. Interest in agile remains strong and shows no signs of slowing. The focus on value streams, customer centricity, and continuous improvement will continue to benefit organizations and increase their competitiveness.

Second, the methodology is likely to evolve and adapt to new trends and practices. Agile has evolved from a pure software development approach to a business philosophy, and similar developments could occur with respect to ART and SAFe. For example, the focus could shift to topics such as artificial intelligence, machine learning, and data analytics as these technologies increasingly impact the way organizations work.

Third, ART and SAFe could also stimulate new forms of collaboration and organization. With their focus on autonomy and self-organization, these approaches could help to break down hierarchical structures and promote more participative and democratic working environments.

Finally, the role of change management may become even more important. As we have seen, the introduction of ART and SAFe represents a profound change for many organizations. In the future, companies that can meet this challenge and effectively bring their employees along on the journey are likely to be the most successful.

In conclusion, the future of ART and SAFe looks exciting and promising. They provide a robust and flexible basis for the continuation of the agile journey and will certainly accompany us for many years to come.

Recommendations for the introduction of ART

Having taken a comprehensive journey through the world of ART and SAFe, it is now time to provide some final recommendations for those considering implementing ART in their organization.

Create awareness and communicate the 'why':

The successful introduction of ART starts with understanding and communicating the reasons why this change is necessary. This should not only be done at the management level, but should include all levels of the organization. Explain the value ART can bring to the organization and how it can help address existing challenges.

Step-by-step implementation:

As with any large-scale change, it is recommended that you take a step-by-step approach. Start with a pilot project or a specific area of the organization and use what you learn to refine the approach before rolling out ART on a larger scale.

Provide appropriate resources and support:

The introduction of ART requires a significant investment in time and resources. This includes training for employees, possibly hiring or appointing Agile coaches, and adapting processes and tools. Ensure that these resources are available and that the necessary support is in place at all levels of the organization.

Cultivate a culture of continuous improvement:

One of the central aspects of ART is continuous improvement. This should be applied not only to product development, but also to the ART process itself. Use retrospective meetings and feedback loops to regularly review and improve the process.

Engage executives:

Management support is critical to the success of ART. Managers should not only support the introduction of ART, but also act as role models and promote the agile mindset throughout the organization.

Finally, it should be noted that each organization is unique, and what works in one organization may not work in another. Therefore, ART should be viewed as a guide rather than a rigid prescription. It is important to adapt the principles and practices to the specific needs and context of your organization. With these recommendations, you will be well equipped to succeed on your ART journey.

Dose ________ for your liver

Printed in the USA
CPSIA information can be obtained
at www.ICGtesting.com
CBHW031145060424
6499CB00012B/543